Praise for *The ABCs of Life*

D0089264

"I am honored to be able to voice my support for both my friend, Byron Garrett, and his powerful book, The ABCs of Life. As an inspirational artist, the messages that run through this book truly hit home for me. This is more than just a self-help book. This is a book that puts you on a path to greatness. Byron's method of dissecting such powerful insight into something as basic as the ABCs makes this an easy yet impactful read. If you truly take the time to digest the messages from The ABCs of Life, you will find yourself inspired, prepared, and filled with purpose."

> **—DONALD LAWRENCE**, Grammy Award-Winning Producer

"Every young person will find here a powerful road map to help realize his or her own God-given potential. Byron Garrett is a dream maker and has spent his life supporting young people and their families—he knows what he's talking about."

> **—MARGUERITE KONDRACKE, former President and CEO, America's Promise Alliance**

"The ABCs of Life will take you on an inspirational journey to reach your highest potential. This book provides a wealth of knowledge for the development of your personal blueprint toward the path to new heights."

> **—MONTA ELLIS**, NBA Player, and **JUANIKA ELLIS**

"I appreciated the valuable reminders in each life lesson and will return to this book many times. The lessons are timeless."
—**STEPHANIE HIRSH**, Executive Director, Learning Forward

"Exceptional... meticulously written, this book is filled with simple principles that will stimulate and activate you to achieve your purpose and goals. The ABCs will definitely empower you!"
—**TICHINA ARNOLD**, Mother, Actress, and Singer

"With more than a decade of securing the well-being of children, my passion was again ignited by The ABCs of Life. The alphabet format may be simple, but the message is nothing short of inspirational. This book is a must read for every man, woman, and child."
—**NICOLE C. DAVIS**, Esq., Chief Counsel, Child and Family Protection Office of the Arizona Attorney General

"Byron Garrett's passion and enthusiasm for raising the next great generation are infectious. His thoughtful wisdom and encouraging outlook will inspire the youth of today to settle for nothing less than success and to savor every moment of the climb up the ladder."
—**ANA CONNERY**, Content Director, *Parenting* magazine and Parenting.com

BYRON V. GARRETT

The
ABCs
of
Life

Words of Wisdom—From A to Z—
for Living Life to the Fullest

◣SCHOLASTIC

NEW YORK • TORONTO • LONDON • AUCKLAND • SYDNEY
MEXICO CITY • NEW DELHI • HONG KONG • BUENOS AIRES

Cover and interior design by Maria Lilja
Illustrations/photographs by Mia Skaili, except as noted; Photodisc (pages 22–25, 42–57);
© Konstantin Sutyagin/Shutterstock, Inc. (page 58); © Ryan DeBerardinis/Shutterstock,
Inc. (page 60); and © Markovka/Shutterstock, Inc. (page 62).
"Order My Steps" composed by Glenn Edward Burleigh. Used by permission.

Acknowledgments

To the One above, who leads, guides, and directs all that I do.

To the one and only GW "MF" Booth, aka Double Deuce, I am a better person because of you.

To my parents, who serve as the compass for my ways and the foundation of my wisdom.

To my brothers, sisters-in-law, and my adopted big sisters (Evelyn, Nicole, CeCe, and Tichina), thanks for your unwavering support and encouragement as I pursue my dreams.

To my nephews, who are constant reminders of why I do what I do; I draw inspiration knowing that you are living your lives to the fullest.

To the Garrett, Scales, Whitsett, and Booth families, as well as my extended family and friends, thanks for always being there and offering your support.

Kudos to my personal advisory board: Phil Clark, Ryan Underwood, Genel Burwell, Tomeka Gross, Stephen Knight, and James Garrett.

Special thanks to my team at Scholastic: Greg, Jennifer, Karine, Dominique, Kyle, Virginia, Patrick, Eileen, Mela, and Maria! You are awesome; it's an honor to partner with you.

My deepest appreciation to the tens of thousands of students, community leaders, parents, educators, and corporations who have used and lived *The ABCs of Life*. I take great pride in the work we have achieved together and look forward to seeing you at the next level.

Table of Contents

Introduction 8

Accept the Challenge 12

Believe in Yourself 14

Choice, Not Chance, Determines Success 16

Develop Your Own Goals and Objectives 18

Expect Failure, but Also Expect Success 20

Fight On, Be Faithful, and Finish What You Start . . . 22

Gravitate Toward Positive, Successful People 24

Harness Everything Within Yourself to Be Happy . . . 26

Initiate the Process 28

Jealousy Gets You Nowhere 30

Keep On Keepin' On 32

Learn How to Learn 34

Mo' Money, Mo' Money, Mo' Money 36

Never, Never, Never Say Never 38

Order Your Steps 40

Practice What You Preach 42

Quit Quitting 44

Respect People 46

Stay Strong to Your Values and Beliefs 48

Travel the Long Road to Equality 50

Utilize Your Network 52

Visualize It 54

Work, Work, Work—'Til Your Work Is Done 56

X-ray Your Own Life 58

Yield to Opportunity 60

Zealously Strive to Achieve 62

Introduction

Greetings! You are embarking upon a journey to unlock your life and unleash the power of leadership, success, and life management. I applaud your efforts. The first step toward getting where you want to be in life is the recognition that there *is* somewhere you want to be. Each of us is obligated to determine, understand, and identify our mission in life. I live by the mantra: Find something in life that you love doing so much that you'd do it for free—but do it so well, you get paid for it.

I've reached the conclusion that every life can be a success story. Life is truly a gift, and we should never take this gift for granted. But there is a distinction between being merely successful and being *highly* successful—being the type of person who makes a significant contribution to family, career, community, or even the world. That's where *The ABCs of Life* comes in. Allow the ABCs to be your how–to guide to living a highly successful life.

As you pursue your dreams, you will no doubt encounter dream makers and dream busters. Dream busters are those who hold you back from achieving your goals and living your life with purpose. I challenge you to seek out dream makers—those who thrive in the midst

> *"The first step toward getting where you want to be in life is the recognition that there is somewhere you want to be."*

of chaos and pursue the positive. Dream makers are visionary change agents who see the world differently than most. When the world pushes them, they dig deep and push back. Dream makers do not accept the status quo and "no" is not part of their vocabulary. They live in the realm of possibility. The essence of a dream maker is the uncanny ability to see beyond present situations while transforming stumbling blocks into stepping-stones and obstacles into opportunities. You, my friend, are destined to live the life of a dream maker.

Accept
the Challenge

> **"Accepting the challenge requires that you take action."**

You must be willing to accept the challenge to be highly successful in life. Most people spend their entire lives waiting for opportunities and great things to happen. Instead of waiting for opportunities, you must take hold of your future and face each day with a spirit of optimism and excitement. You must make the opportunities happen—and recognize each chance to do so.

I remember my parents telling me as a child that the early bird gets the worm. This virtue still holds true. No matter your station in life, begin to accept the challenge as soon as the sun begins to rise each day. Time waits for no one—so there's no time for hesitation and no time for second-guessing yourself.

You'll encounter plenty of people throughout life who will second-guess you. Don't join them. Leave minor details to those who live minor lives. You are on the verge of achieving greatness. Embrace it and make this your reality.

Accepting the challenge requires that you take action. Whether it's a baby step, a hop, a jump, or a giant leap, begin each new day with the desire to excel and a passion for greatness. Without question, "accept" is an action word. You must accept the challenge, adopting the positive mindset that it's a brand new day, and that this new day is filled with opportunities, sometimes disguised as obstacles. Know you are going to make it happen. Begin today. **Accept the challenge.**

Believe
in Yourself

> **"To live a meaningful life, you must find something you believe in wholeheartedly."**

During college, I took classes that dealt with non-profit management. One of the most important lessons I learned was the concept of finding a cause that you believe in with all your heart. One of my professors said that you must demonstrate your belief by giving to the cause. Highly effective people are those who operate in areas where they possess great belief.

A good salesperson believes in his or her product. A great salesperson not only believes in the product but also exudes passion and purpose connected to the product. To live a meaningful life, you must find something you believe in wholeheartedly. For parents, this may be creating a quality life for a family. For an athlete, knowing that with enough focus and conditioning one will excel in a sport. For teachers, this is probably the belief that all students can learn. For students, it's believing that you have the ability to earn an A or a B instead of settling for a C. Whatever you believe in, recognize it's the *belief* that keeps you going when you are tired, weary, and worn down. This belief lifts you when others put you down and gives you the courage to try again when it appears you've fallen short. This kind of passionate belief inspires others to believe as well.

To live a highly successful life, you must believe in yourself. *You* are your primary reason for success. You are the agent of your own success—and you must exude a passion for your purpose. If you are not strong and determined, you will have great difficulty getting others to believe in you. **Believe in yourself.**

Choice,
Not Chance,
Determines
Success

Success is all about the choices you make. Average people take random chances. Then, they waste time making excuses for what they have or have not accomplished in life. You have the opportunity to live your life as you'd like to, but you have to take ownership of the decisions you make, good and bad. Stop making excuses; don't fall into the "Shoulda-Coulda-Woulda" syndrome.

Shift your concentration from merely taking a chance to creating a plan and making the right choice. While we all need to take a chance every now and then, it is important to remember that chances are often random, like the luck of the draw. Choices, on the other hand, require preparation in order to be ready and informed to make the right decision. Take ownership of your world with the understanding that you are the captain of your ship on the sea of life. If the boat sinks, it usually has nothing to do with

> **"You have to take ownership of the decisions you make, good and bad."**

the people or events in your past. It has more to do with the choices you've made to get you to where you are now—in the moment. In life, things may not have worked as you planned, yet you make the choice to eke out a living or to thrive. Make your experiences count. Let all that has gone right or wrong inform you as you make choices to achieve your goals and help you envision what is possible. You are only limited by your ability to think beyond your current reality and look into the realm of possibility.

The ability to make excellent choices is the cornerstone of a highly successful person. Rather than wallow in the bad choices I've made in the past, I focus on my future knowing that, though I may have failed, I am not a failure. Every time you dwell on your past, you are taking your eyes off your future. **Choice, not chance, determines success.**

Develop
Your Own Goals & Objectives

I n today's society, you have the opportunity to dictate, determine, and decide what happens in your life. Numerous factors have an impact on your life—especially in childhood. However, when you reach age 18, life begins to operate differently. You move into an arena where you must develop your own goals and objectives. No longer can you rely upon others to lead, guide, and direct you. You should begin positioning yourself to be a highly successful person.

> **"Begin today by writing down your 1-month, 1-year, 5-year, and lifelong goals."**

So often, you follow the directions that your parents, teachers, or others have set for you. They are there to lead and guide you as you learn to create your own plans. No matter your background, however, at some point you have to take charge of your own destiny. You must develop your own goals and objectives to help you navigate schoolwork, friendships, and all kinds of activities.

If you do not know where you are going and you have no plan in mind, the road will lead you nowhere. In other words, if you fail to plan, you are planning to fail. So, begin today by writing down your 1-month, 1-year, 5-year, and lifelong goals. Success does not happen overnight, but it does happen over time. Begin to plot, plan, and strategize for your future. Remember, at the end of the day, you are held accountable for your actions. **Develop your own goals and objectives.**

Expect
Failure,
but Also
Expect
Success

> **"Through practice you build the skill, ability, and confidence to deliver when the key moment arises."**

There are times in life when we must surrender to the reality that you have human limitations. Occasionally, we may try something over and over again only to be met with continued defeat and failure. Though I don't expect everything to be a failure, I do understand that in order to achieve greatly, I may fail greatly.

Give thought to the millions of people who know how to ride a bike. And out of those, only a small percentage hopped right on without training wheels and rode immediately. If you are like me, you fell off time and time again. But you don't know how to ride the bike because you fell off, you know how to ride because you got back on. Life is the same way; it's not a matter of failure, but of discovering the power of getting back up and starting again. Through practice you build the skill, ability, and confidence to deliver when the key moment arises.

As you proceed through life, do not become discouraged by failure but look at it as a unique opportunity. Though I have failed or fallen short often, it is during my failures that I have increased my knowledge, determination, and perseverance to exceed even my own expectations. Though some will see failure, if you see instead an opportunity to rise with a spirit of determination combined with sheer willpower, you are a success waiting to happen! You can **expect failure, but also expect success.**

Fight On,
Be Faithful
& Finish What You Start

> **"You must work twice as hard and believe twice as much as anyone else to get where you want to go."**

Many people start things in life but never finish. I have great difficulty understanding why someone would start something and then lose sight of the goal. As we strive, we hope to accomplish great things, but we too often allow disappointments and setbacks—and maybe the pursuit of too many things—to cloud our judgment. I refuse to allow others to deter me from my goal. When I'm centered on something, I am going to stick with it until it's finished.

Newton's law shows us that an object in motion will continue to be in motion until acted upon by an opposite force. I know firsthand that the force of negativity often seems greater than the force of positivity. Therefore, you must work twice as hard and believe twice as much as anyone else to get where you want to go. You have the ability to deliver. **Fight on, be faithful, and finish what you start.**

Gravitate

Toward Positive, Successful People

> **"Your challenge is to gravitate toward people who have a healthy, positive thought process."**

Some people suffer from "stinking thinking." Stinking thinking is the state of mind of negative thinkers. Their thinking process just plain stinks. You may suffer from this thought process yourself or sense it in the people around you. In your effort to become highly successful, your challenge is to gravitate toward people who have a healthy, positive thought process.

As a boy, I was told that people could tell a lot about you by the company you keep. Who do you have around you? If they are not positive people who are about something, then you need to consider weeding them out of your life. It doesn't matter if it is your husband or wife, boss, neighbor, or best friend; if the people you spend time with do not have a positive outlook on life, think about changing the company you keep.

You need to surround yourself with people who have a positive mindset, who, like you, strive to achieve things. Do you know how great it would be to spend most of your time around people who think positively? It would transform your life. You will be more vibrant, more energetic, and more excited instead of feeling down in the dumps. Dumps are filled with garbage—which stinks. There is no time for "stinking thinking." Resist getting caught up in the same old stuff again and again. Break the cycle. **Gravitate toward positive, successful people.**

Harness

Everything Within Yourself to Be Happy

The ability to channel your energy, time, and attention in a singular direction is the premise of harnessing everything within you. Throughout all that happens in life, no matter the situation or circumstance, you must harness all that you have and be focused. All too often we want the quick-fix solutions and easy gains. Nothing in life worth having comes easy. Thus, you have to stay committed and be determined to reach your goal.

> **"Throughout all that happens in life, no matter the situation or circumstance, you must harness all that you have to be focused."**

I remember the film *The Karate Kid*, where the martial arts teacher is striving to teach "Daniel-san" to protect himself. In the final round of the championship, Daniel sustains an injury and has full use of only one leg. But recalling the words of his teacher, "Daniel-san, focus," Daniel is able to use his one leg in a crane motion to defeat his opponent. Whatever it is you strive to do in life, focus!

Harness the energy within yourself to be successful.

Happiness is something money cannot afford. If it were, it would be traded on the New York Stock Exchange. Many squander their fortunes by buying things in hopes of attaining happiness. To find real happiness, you need to look inward not outward, beginning with yourself and not others. **Harness everything within yourself to be happy.**

Initiate
the **Process**

Have you ever wondered why it seems some people get all the breaks and you are still struggling to just maintain? I would offer that they don't get all the breaks, but rather somewhere along the way they initiate the process. If you want to do better in school, on the job, or in your community, you must continually seek opportunities to do so.

> **"Stop waiting for others to bestow good things upon you. Success doesn't come to you; you've got to go get it."**

The word "initiate" requires you to take the first step. Instead of waiting for something to fall from the sky or all of the planets to align, you need to get your butt in motion. Why put off 'til tomorrow what you can do today? Initiate the process! You have the ability, the knowledge, the wisdom, and the determination to do great things. Do yourself a favor: Stop waiting for others to bestow good things upon you. Success doesn't come to you; you've got to go get it. Step out in faith and courage by making it happen—today. Yesterday is a memory, and tomorrow is still a dream. Today is the first day of the rest of your life, and you can start today to make tomorrow's dream a reality. **Initiate the process!**

Jealousy
Gets You Nowhere

> **"People who are busy unlocking the power of their life don't have time to be jealous."**

Throughout school you probably mastered the concept of being jealous. Jealous of her hair. Jealous of her skills on the field. Jealous of him because he dates the girl you like. Jealous because he gets all the digits. Jealous of their lives. Well, the reality is this: Jealously gets you nowhere. To be successful, you must take action, rather than become paralyzed by jealousy or focus on what someone else has acquired or accomplished.

At some point, you need to stop being a "hater." You know these kinds of people. Haters are the ones who always have something discouraging to say or comment negatively about everyone else. Stop spending your time and energy being jealous of someone else's life. Stop simply comparing the "haves" and "have-nots." While you waste your energy wondering why you are a have-not, you could just as well be pursuing what you want to do.

People who are busy unlocking the power of their life don't have time to be jealous. There is action to be taken and work to be done. Start being the most positive person you know. Embrace the concept of you and understand that no one can beat you at being you. **Jealousy gets you nowhere.**

Keep On
Keepin' On

There will be times in life when you feel like throwing in the towel. You are ready to give up, give in, and give out. Don't do it. In the poem "Mother to Son" by Langston Hughes, a mother tells her son about trials and tribulations he may encounter in life. She also tells him that with everything that comes his way, not to sit and rest because he's got work to do. The mother says that she has to keep trying, even when there seems to be no end in sight, even when

> **"If you truly desire to be highly successful, there will be people and things you'll have to say no to on your journey."**

things seem hopeless, and that the boy will need to do the same.

I don't know your situation or your circumstance, but I do know you didn't come this far to stop. My own ultimate goal is to ascend above the clouds, and I truly understand you cannot "sit" your way into heaven. In fact, you cannot progress by sitting your way anywhere. You have to keep on keepin' on, no matter how many negative habits, negative folks, and negative feelings you encounter along the way.

If you truly desire to be highly successful, there will be people and things you'll have to say no to on your journey. It doesn't mean you are being unkind, or that you are looking down upon people, you simply realize that you need to focus on forward motion. Only you know what it will take for you to make it, but to get there, you know what you need to do: **Keep on keepin' on!**

Learn

How to Learn

As a child, I was always advised to learn something new every day. Each and every morning as I prepared to go to school, my mother would say, "Learn something new today." At the end of the day, Mom would do a status check: "What did you learn today?" I quickly learned that saying "nothing" was far from the right answer.

If you go to school, work, or anywhere for roughly 7 to 9 hours and you cannot explain or quantify what you learned,

"You only get out of something what you put into it."

something is terribly wrong. Over the course of my life, I have spent approximately 22 years enrolled in formal education. In each of these settings I strived to give it my all because, it is true: You only get out of something what you put into it.

I profess to be a lifelong learner. This does not mean I plan to be enrolled in school for the rest of my life. However, in order to be effective, I have to continue to learn, grow, and prosper each and every day.

Someone once told me that learning seemed too much like work. Call it what you want to, but never underestimate the importance of learning—formal or informal, street or otherwise. Learning is critical to your success. The people who don't get passed by are the ones who know how to learn—and keep learning new things. The more you learn, the more you earn; the more you know, the more you grow. So, **learn how to learn!**

Mo' Money, Mo' Money, Mo' Money

The world we live in seems to revolve around "mo' money, mo' money, mo' money." However, Sean Combs penned these lyrics, which may strike a chord: "... it's like the more money we come across, the more problems we see." While money is important, it can't solve all your problems—and sometimes it creates them! I jokingly tell people that I speak two languages—money and English. If you'd like to speak French let's discuss francs, if you'd prefer to speak Spanish, we'll discuss pesos, and if you want to speak the language of hip-hop culture, then let's begin with the "benjamins." Money is right up there with oxygen; it seems you just cannot live, breathe, or die without it.

As you know, I contend that to be successful you should find something in life that you love doing. Find something you'd do for free—but do it so well you

"Find something you'd do for free—but do it so well you get paid for it."

get paid for it. Thus, it becomes an issue of mission over money, and often if you are on target with your mission, the money will follow. Before you start dreaming about the big bucks, recognize that some careers offer better compensation while others offer peace of mind. If you decide to be an artist to feed your soul, know that you might need to do something else to fill your wallet. But being positive will make that more likely to happen.

Remember, money should not be your master. You should measure your worth based upon what's inside your head and heart, not what's parked in your driveway or hanging in your closet. Live your life with a purpose. Concentrate on the mission, not **mo' money, mo' money, mo' money.**

Never, Never, Never Say Never

When I was in college, it was popular to ask people what they would or would not do for money. Though I personally have yet to do anything out of the norm, the reality is unless you are exiting the earth in the next few minutes, you cannot truly say what you will or will not ever do. I do believe you have to live a life of principle. But when I speak of never, never, never saying never, I'm referring to having that natural instinct to rise in the

> **"No matter what obstacles stand in your path, your success depends on your believing in yourself and in your future."**

midst of adversity and do what it takes to succeed.

So many have failed to realize their dreams, not due to a lack of potential but a lack of determination and hope in the future. No matter what obstacles stand in your path, your success depends on your believing in yourself and in your future. It may be easy to give in to self-doubt when you lack a belief in yourself and lose sight of your dreams. However, it is your duty to yourself to never say never. That which was not possible today may very well be possible tomorrow. Can you imagine giving up right now as you're going down life's highway only to find that the goal you were seeking was just around the corner?

This is your life. Stay true to your dreams and principles, and never say it can't be done. Do not accept "no" for an answer, do not give up hope, and **never, never, never say never.**

Order
Your Steps

As a person of strong faith, I utilize gospel music as a vehicle to help me transcend the world within which I live. One song that has encouraged me is entitled "Order My Steps." This song has always had a humbling effect on the very core of who I claim to be. I know without question that it is by God's grace that I am who I am. For nothing I have achieved or attained was gained by my effort alone, but through the wisdom, gifts, and talents I've been

> **"At some point you must recognize that the world is larger than you. It is my firm belief that a higher power guides all that we do."**

blessed with in my life. Indeed, each of us has been blessed with gifts and potential. And we owe it to ourselves and to our Creator to live up to that potential.

At some point you must recognize that the world is larger than you. It is my firm belief that a higher power guides all that we do. I believe that we should pray daily, seeking wisdom and guidance for our steps to be ordered so we might fulfill the destiny awaiting each of us.

Strive for meaning in your life. Understand that there is a design for your life. Whether you like it or not, you are designed to be a contributor to a greater good, so **order your steps.**

"Order my steps in your word,
dear Lord,
Lead me, guide me, every day.
Send your anointing, Father,
I pray...
Please, order my steps in
your word."

Practice
What You
Preach

> **"Instead of merely telling someone how to be a better person, your own life and actions should serve as a model."**

During my tenure as a school principal, I learned the value of "walking the walk and talking the talk." Children have this amazing ability to remind us that we, too, have expectations to live up to. It's one thing to set, establish, or identify a model for others to live by. It is another thing completely to actually live that life. My elders in church referred to this as living the life you sing about. Of course, that was before 50 Cent and Lil' Kim came on the scene.

The fact of the matter is you should spend more time practicing than preaching. In other words, most of your time should be spent doing, not telling. Instead of merely telling someone how to be a better person, your own life and actions should serve as a model. I'm always cautious of people who are "flossing and glossing, fronting and stunting." They seem like they have "swag," but they truly lack substance.

You should be living by the same high standards you expect others to live by. You should understand that a person of character is one who does the right thing even when no one else is looking. A person of high self-worth embraces the Golden Rule and goes beyond it—treating others *better* than he or she would like to be treated. Let your actions speak for themselves. **Practice what you preach.**

Quit
Quitting

Quit quitting! Quitters never win and winners never quit. We live in a society where you can take medication for almost anything you can imagine. I wish there were a medicine to force you to stick to your dreams and hold fast to your future, but it's yet to be invented. I meet so many people who have become so discouraged that they've started giving up on life. The sparkle and smiles that used to highlight

> **"While success may not come overnight, it does come over time."**

their faces have been replaced with frowns and frustration.

My friend, you have to understand that you can never win if you quit. You are just getting started. While success may not come overnight, it does come over time. You can't imagine the number of great successes throughout history who were on the verge of calling it quits. Yet, they achieved greatness because they never quit. I'm not saying it will not be tough or difficult. It will. It's during those very times when it seems the world has turned its back on you that you have to stay the course, knowing that the only thing standing between you and achievement is a temporary setback.

Dig in, suck it up, and get your rear in gear. Great things are already in motion, awaiting your arrival. You've come this far, so don't stop now. **Quit quitting!**

Respect People

> **"You should become a person who commands respect because you have earned it—and because you give it."**

The issue of respect is central to leadership and success in life. Some people believe you earn respect, while others believe you demand it. The reality is just because you have a title doesn't mean people respect you. In fact, sometimes people don't even respect the title or the position you hold.

You should become a person who commands respect because you have earned it—and because you give it. I have encountered people from all walks of life. Those who have moved from "Losing Lane" to "Luxury Avenue" and from "Luxury Avenue" to "Losing Lane." In the final analysis, I respect people based upon their skills, talents, and achievements—and upon their principles. How you live and how you treat others shows your character.

No matter your vocation or avocation, you should desire to be a person who is respected by those with whom you live, work, and play. Ultimately, a person worthy of respect is one who also respects others. I will be the first to say that I'm not usually concerned with whether people like me as long as they respect me. An *excellent* leader is liked and well respected. You have the ability to achieve both, especially when you remember that you have to bring some respect to get some respect— when and where it is due. **Respect people.**

Stay Strong

to **Your Values** & **Beliefs**

> **"You have to stay true to those principles that guide what you do and govern who you are in life."**

Society advances at such a rapid rate, I'm amazed people are able to keep up. It's so easy and convenient to follow the latest trend or adopt the current buzz words of the day. I would caution you not to get so caught up with the "here and now" that you forget about the "there and then."

A key to success in life is staying strong and remaining true to your core values and beliefs. You have to stay true to those principles that guide what you do and govern who you are in life. I read a quote once that went, "What is popular is not always right, and what is right is not always popular." Popular or not, your principles must guide you.

I hope you have an internal compass that provides direction for your life. When you are in the midst of difficult times, when you might consider selling out or compromising your beliefs, it's your internal compass that says, "There is danger ahead; steer clear." Every morning, you have to look yourself in the mirror and determine whether you are happy with who you are and who you are becoming.

Your values and beliefs will serve you well if you live by them! If you do, you'll find that in spite of your situation or circumstance, you can smile at the person you see in the mirror without feeling ashamed or guilty for anything. **Stay strong to your values and beliefs.**

Travel

the **Long Road**
to **Equality**

"Don't get caught up in the concept of the 'haves' and 'have-nots.'"

Many would like to think that society now offers a level playing field. I have traveled extensively across the United States and around the globe and have discovered this simply is not the case. Whether it is gender, religion, intelligence, age, weight, sexual preference, socio-economic status or any other classification, the world in which we live is not an equal place. You need to recognize this and move forward.

Don't get caught up in the concept of the "haves" and "have-nots." While it is very important to acknowledge that life is not always fair, the time you spend justifying your situation could just as well be spent moving from point A to Z. I'm not saying disregard the inequalities in life, rather acknowledge them for what they are and prepare to move forward even in the midst of adversity.

Some people will hate on you no matter what you do, who you are, or where you are from. How you respond to the negativity—the "hateration" (to borrow a word from Mary J. Blige)—is what's of vital significance. Let your haters be your motivators. I refuse to allow someone else to define who I am or limit where I can go. I'm just not going to do it.

The road to equality is long and hard. So what else is new? What are you going to do—stop? I think not. Instead, enjoy the sweetness of victory. Through your success you will help make the world more equal. It may not be easy, but it will be worth it to **travel the long road to equality.**

Utilize
Your Network

Never underestimate the value of networking. I attribute a significant portion of my success to a solid network. While you may not personally have an outstanding network as of yet, don't hesitate to seek a mentor or advisor and tap into his or her network.

As a student in high school and as an undergrad, I was very involved in Junior Achievement. After completing a summer internship, I maintained contact with people whom I encountered from the national staff. One of my key advisors, even now, is a woman named Evelyn, who agreed to mentor me during my participation. Evelyn would position me to take advantage of great opportunities. Though I may not have understood the value or purpose, she would make sure I was ready and prepared to benefit from each opportunity.

> **"While you may not personally have an outstanding network as of yet, don't hesitate to seek a mentor or advisor and tap into his or her network."**

From that network, I grew a network with celebrities, dignitaries, elected officials, and corporate executives. Evelyn and I have maintained contact for more than two decades, and we continue to access each other's network as needed.

There's an old saying, "It's not what you know, it's who you know." Knowledge is key, but so is a network. Whose contact list are you in? Who is in your circle of influence? Your network should be full of contacts, direct and indirect. If the theory of six degrees of separation is true, and if you are doing what you should be doing, you may be only six degrees away from the very person or resource you need access to. So, **utilize your network.**

Visualize It

> **"You have to be able not only to create a vision for your life but also be able to articulate it and enroll others in that vision."**

Only when you see it, can you be it. The ability to be a visionary is a powerful tool. I consider it one of the greatest keys to success, yet one of the least talked about. You have to be able not only to create a vision for your life but also be able to articulate it and enroll others in that vision.

When I started Progressive Schools, I could tell you what the classroom, cafeteria, staff, students, and buses looked like. Though I could not physically show others, I could certainly share the vision verbally and enroll them in the concept to ensure its success.

How do you know what success looks like when you attain it? You have to have some picture within your mind and indication in your heart about the vision for your life. The Word says, "Write the vision and make it plain that men may read it and run with it!" It also says, "Without vision, the people perish."

You'll be surprised by how motivated you will be and how inspiring you can be to others when you can see success unfold before your very eyes. **Visualize it!**

Work,
Work, Work—
'Til Your
Work Is Done

"Your success depends on your willingness to actually do the work."

Your success depends on your willingness to actually do the work. This may mean getting your hands dirty or breaking a sweat—whatever it takes to get the job done. You have to be willing to do the work.

You also can't expect other people to drop what they are doing and begin to help you with your work. It doesn't quite work that way. It's no surprise that people don't usually get involved with the great work you're doing until they realize it's a success in the making. Thus, you can't count on others to do your work. If they pitch in and help out, wonderful—if they don't, you need to make sure that your show is going strong.

All of the ventures I've pursued in business and advanced education required that I work twice as hard and twice as long as others. You have to be willing to do today what others won't so you can have a tomorrow that others never will. You simply have to be willing to do the work, no matter how long or how hard it is. Just as there is no shortcut to greatness, there is no shortcut to getting the job done. You must **work, work, work— 'til your work is done.**

X-ray
Your Own Life

> **"Getting to where you want to be can be as simple as minding and tending to your own business."**

Many people spend their lives on the verge of success. Getting to where you want to be can be as simple as minding and tending to your own business. Instead of analyzing the lives of others—what they have, what their motivations are, and so on—you should be "X-raying" your own life in order to improve upon it.

As a student and later a school administrator, I quickly discovered that the students who were in trouble most frequently were those who could not or would not tend to their own business. It's human nature to be curious and inquisitive—and to dream. But given the dreams *you* have, your time should be spent inquiring about how to make *them* come true. Otherwise you'll be like most, sitting on the sidelines of life waiting to get into the game.

In essence, you have 24 hours in a day—12 hours to mind your business and 12 hours to take care of your business, which leaves *zero* time for anybody else's business. The game has already started. Get with the program and **X-ray your own life.**

Yield
to **Opportunity**

Occasionally, I find myself rushing from one project or activity to another. In the midst of my haste, I may miss significant opportunities staring me right in the face. While I encourage your enthusiasm for success in general, remember to allow time to take advantage of what life has to offer in the present.

I have to remind myself sometimes to slow down and enjoy the ride, allowing time for great things to develop along the way. Of course, it's one thing

> **"As you structure your life plan, know that you will encounter detours along the highway to success."**

to recognize you need to yield to opportunity; it's another to actually do it.

As you structure your life plan, know that you will encounter detours along the highway to success. These may take you five days out of your way to accomplishing your goals, or you may end up spending five years heading in a slightly different direction but with your eyes still fixed upon the original prize. There is no right or wrong. Life often surprises us with some of the most beautiful blessings when we yield to opportunity.

It's like that wise expression: "Take time to stop and smell the roses." If your life is too carefully planned and rigidly executed, you may not have the time to follow up on or take advantage of a wonderful opportunity along the way. It may initially seem like this detour is taking you off course, but it more than likely will serve to propel you further into the future you have envisioned. **Yield to opportunity!**

Zealously
Strive to Achieve

> **"With every fiber of your being, you have to know that you have what it takes to make it."**

When it comes to your life, I wish you passion, patience, and personal power as you strive to achieve your goals. In order to do this—to place all your ABCs of life in the proper perspective—you must zealously strive to achieve.

With every fiber of your being, you have to know that you have what it takes to make it. You should be zealous in all that you do. Pursue your dreams like a child let loose in a toy store; you never know when your mother will say it's time to go, so dive in and try out all you can while you can.

You are destined for great things, and your future is growing brighter by the second. Allow tenacity to be your fuel, passion to be your engine, and your zeal to be the oil that keeps the motor running. You will live a prosperous life when you use everything within you to **zealously strive to achieve.**

"You, my friend,
are destined to live the life
of a dream maker."